Race To

Contents

	Page
Space Race	2-3
First satellite	4
First spacewalk	5
Getting ready	6-7
Spacesuits	8-9
Rockets	10-11
Going to the Moon	12-13
Landing	14-15
Back to Earth	16

written by John Lockyer

In the beginning, Russia was winning the race. It was the first to put a satellite in space. The satellite was called Sputnik. It looked like a shiny basketball, and it sent back radio messages as it flew around Earth.

Sputnik launch 1957

After that, Russia launched many other spacecraft. The first man and the first woman in space were from Russia. A Russian was the first person to walk in space.

The United States was behind in the Space Race, but it was catching up fast. Astronauts were sent into space many times to learn all they could. They got useful new information each time.

spacecraft

They worked out the best way to fly their spacecraft, and how to join up with others. Astronauts became better at spacewalking.

There is no air in space, so astronauts need a spacesuit when they are outside the spacecraft. A backpack on the spacesuit holds oxygen for the astronaut to breathe.

spacesuit

A spacesuit is hard and heavy to work in. It's like being inside a big metal balloon, but it keeps the astronaut safe from the heat and cold in space.

The United States was first to build a rocket that was powerful enough to send people up to the Moon and back. It was called Saturn V. Thirty-two Saturn rockets were built.

Saturn V rocket

The first rockets were tested without a crew. Then more were tested with crews. Other Saturn rockets were used to launch and test the spacecraft that would land on the Moon.

In July 1969, a Saturn V rocket launched the Apollo 11 spacecraft. The crew were Neil Armstrong, Michael Collins and Buzz Aldrin. Two of these men became the first people to land on the Moon.

Apollo 11 crew

The main spacecraft was called Columbia. It carried a Moon lander called the Eagle. When Columbia got close to the Moon, Michael Collins stayed aboard while Neil Armstrong and Buzz Aldrin flew down in the Eagle.

Millions of people on Earth heard Neil Armstrong say, "The Eagle has landed." They watched on television as he and Buzz Aldrin climbed down a ladder and stood on the Moon.

first man on the moon

They put up the United States flag, collected some rocks, and took photos of the Moon's surface. After two and a half hours, they went back to Columbia and flew back to Earth.

Four days later, Columbia landed by splashing down in the Pacific Ocean. The astronauts were safely back on Earth. The race to the Moon was over.

PIONEER VAL...

PARTS OF THE BODY

TRINA LAWRENCE

Look at my hands.

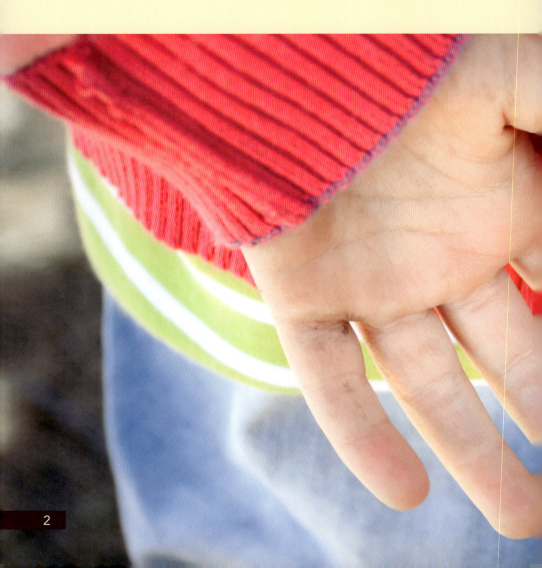

Look at my fingers.

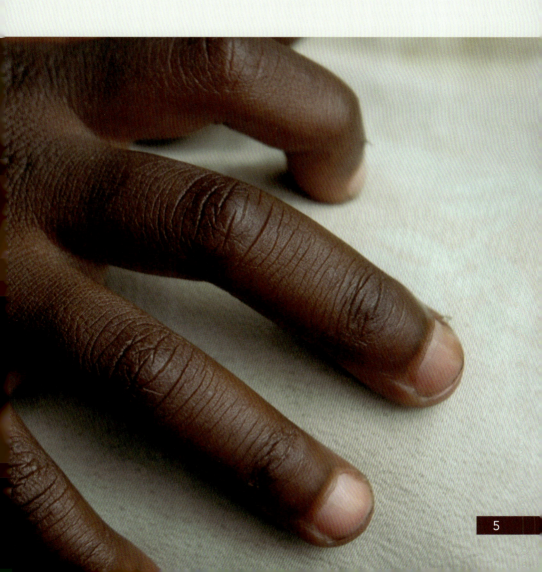

Look at my feet.

Look at my toes.

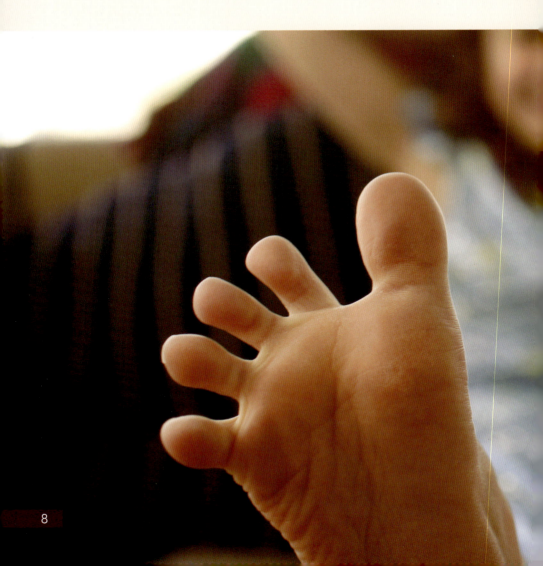

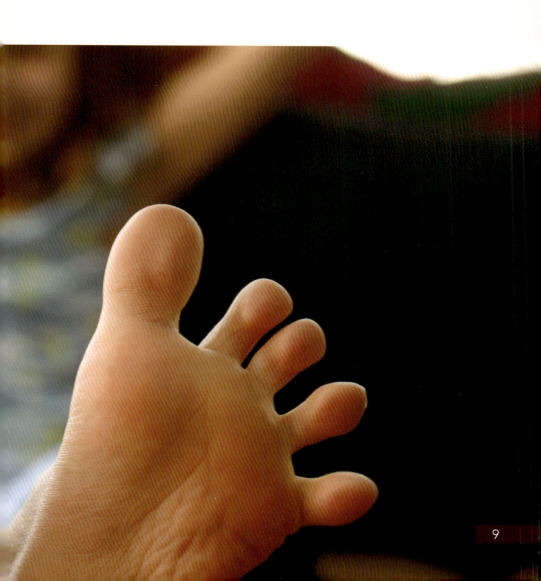

Look at my eyes.

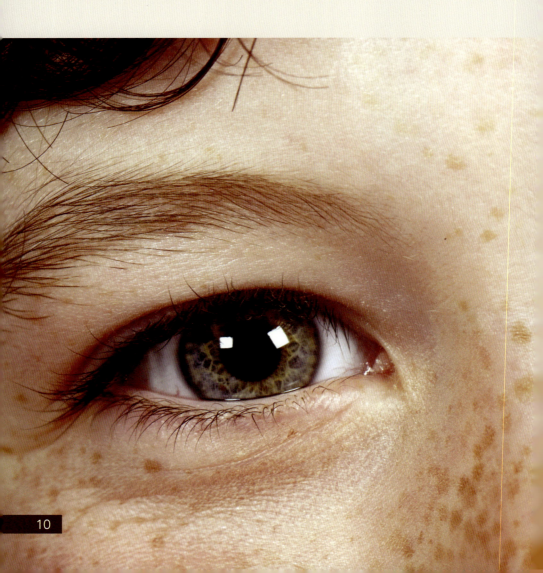

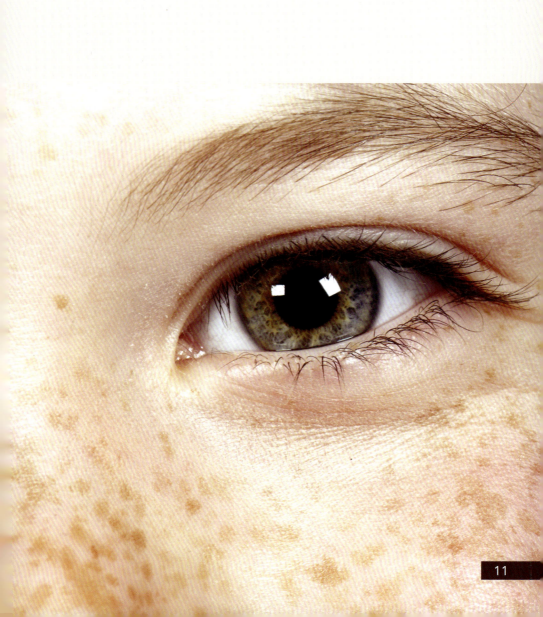

Look at my nose.

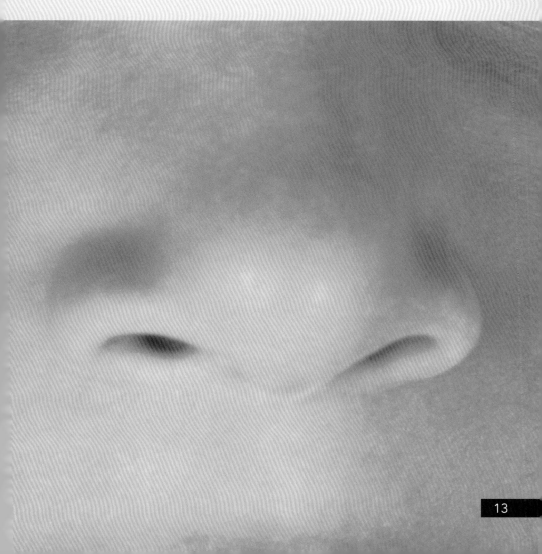

Look at my mouth.

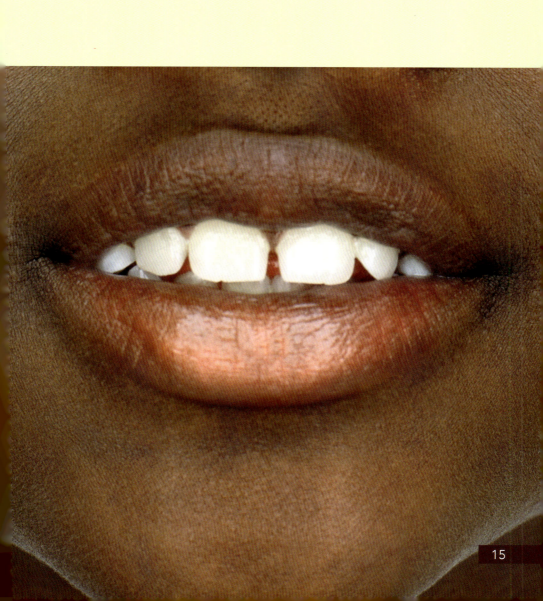

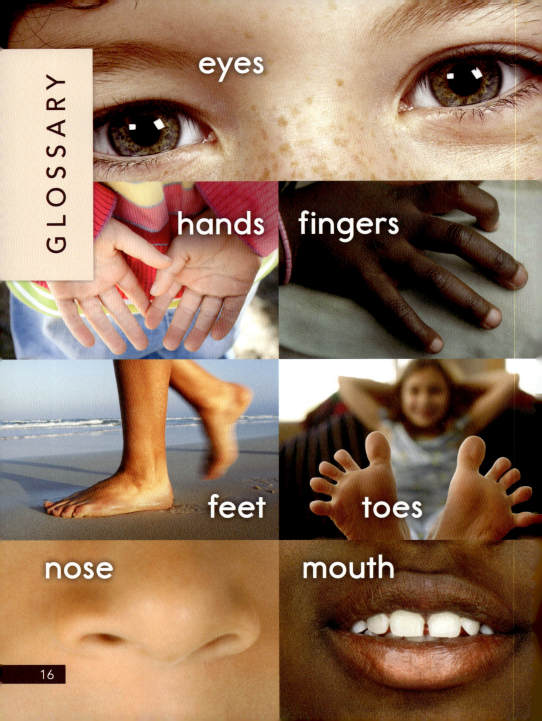